MADE IN THE
U.S.A.

GUITARS
From Start to Finish

Samuel G. Woods

**Photographs by
Gale Zucker**

BLACKBIRCH PRESS, INC.
WOODBRIDGE, CONNECTICUT

Special Thanks
The publisher would like to thank Dick Boak, Director
of Artist Relations, Martin Guitar Company, for his valuable
help and cooperation in putting this book together.

Published by Blackbirch Press, Inc.
260 Amity Road
Woodbridge, CT 06525

e-mail: staff@blackbirch.com
Web site: www.blackbirch.com

©1999 by Blackbirch Press, Inc.
First Edition

Printed in Singapore

10 9 8 7 6 5 4 3 2 1

Photo Credits: All photos by Gale Zucker, except pages 3
(photo by Robert Knight, courtesy of Martin Guitar Co.), 7
(guitar), 14–15, 23 (guitar), 29 courtesy Martin Guitar Company.

Library of Congress Cataloging-in-Publication Data
Woods, Samuel.
Guitars from start to finish / Samuel G. Woods : photographs by Gale Zucker.
   p.   cm. — (Made in the U.S.A.)
   Includes bibliographical references and index.
   Summary: Explains how an acoustic guitar is made, from the choosing of
the wood, through the gluing, side bending, scalloping, purfling, and creation
of special designs, until the strings are added.
   ISBN 1-56711-392-3
   1. Guitar—Construction—Juvenile literature. [1. Guitar—Construction]
I. Zucker, Gale, ill. II. Title. III. Series
ML1015.G9W66   1999
787.87'1923—dc21   99-13861
                                                          CIP
                                                          AC

Contents

If you like music, you've probably seen or played a guitar. If you've heard a skilled musician play, you also know how wonderful a guitar can sound!

Guitars are more than instruments. They are also fine examples of woodworking design and craftsmanship.

There are two basic kinds of guitars. Electric guitars are wired with equipment that amplifies the sounds they make. Acoustic or "classical" guitars have deeper, hollow bodies that echo and vibrate to produce rich, warm sounds.

This is the story of how an acoustic guitar is made.

Stephen Stills

300 Steps

The Martin Guitar Company in Nazareth, Pennsylvania, has been making guitars for more than 166 years. Today, the company produces about 50,000 guitars per year. That's an average of about 150-200 per day.

Each guitar requires more than 300 separate steps to be completed. All together, one guitar takes an average of 3-6 months to make.

Choosing the Wood

Acoustic guitars are made mostly out of wood. Different kinds of wood are used on different parts of each guitar. Some woods are best for producing deep, rich sounds. Other woods produce crisper, higher sounds best. Martin guitars are made mostly from mahogany, rosewood, and spruce.

First, the wood must be chosen and inspected. Before a piece is chosen, it is checked for quality, grain, color, and other features. The best pieces are matched up with each other.

Right: Raw spruce sheets.
Below: Matching and selecting mahogany sides and backs.

Removing rosewood sides from the air-drying stacks.

Mahogany pieces used for guitar backs are glued and held in a wheel-like clamping machine called a glue caul.

Gluing

After pieces are matched, the pairs are glued together. They are clamped and held on a large wheel-like series of clamps called a glue caul.

When guitar backs are glued, a decorative inlay strip is inserted in between the two pieces. Inlay strips come in many unique and beautiful patterns. Some are very fancy.

Once the glue has dried, the large, rectangular pieces are cut into the curvy shape needed for the front or back of a guitar.

*Trimming the end of
a back inlay strip.*

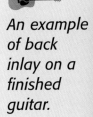

*An example
of back
inlay on a
finished
guitar.*

7

Side Bending

Indian rosewood is used for the sides of each guitar. Long, thin planks are delivered to the bending department. There, they are carefully molded over a hot pipe or bending iron to fit the shape of each body.

For bending, a strip is first sprayed with water, then heated on an iron.

As the wood heats, it is gently bent into shape.

More water is sprayed before further bending is done.

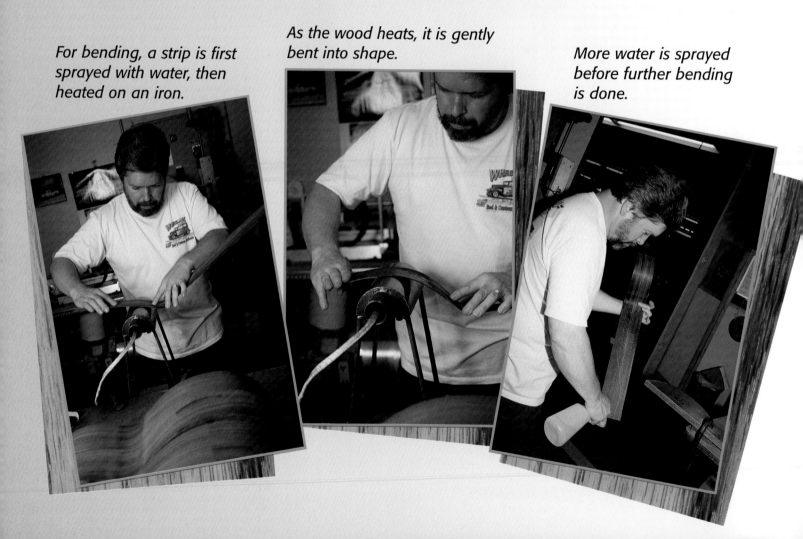

Each piece must fit the master mold exactly.

Bending the rosewood pieces by hand requires a highly skilled craftsperson. After spraying each piece with water, the wood is placed on an iron that is heated to more than 400 degrees F (204° C). As the misted wood heats, the steam helps to bend it. The side piece is checked after each bend to make sure it follows the mold pattern exactly.

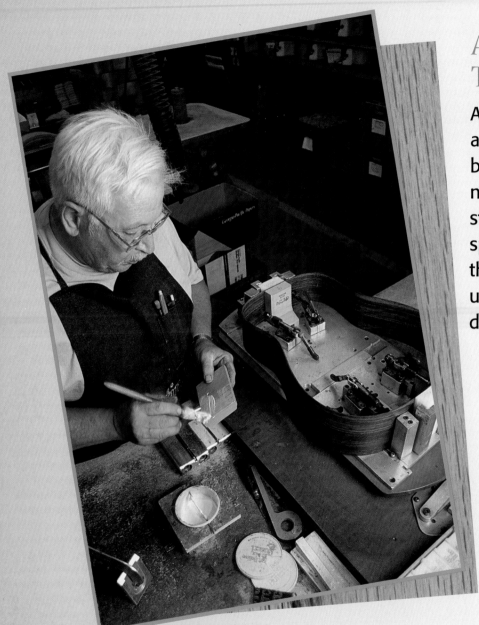

A Guitar Takes Shape

After the sides are bent, they are glued together. Mahogany blocks are attached at the neck base and bottom to add strength and support. A special clamp and mold hold the guitar's rim together under pressure as the glue dries.

Mahogany blocks are glued on the inside where the two side pieces come together. These blocks offer strength and support.

♪ Sidenotes

Some of the world's most famous musicians have used Martin guitars. Among them are: John Lennon and Paul McCartney, Eric Clapton, Paul Simon, Bob Dylan, Elvis Presley, Jimi Hendrix, Joan Baez, Willie Nelson, and Marty Stuart.

A special clamp holds all the pieces tightly in place as the glue dries.

11

Clothespins are attached to the kerfed (notched) lining that is applied to the top and bottom of the body frame.

Special "Kerfed" Lining

A special lining is added to the inside of the guitar's rim. The lining is made of kerfed (notched) Spanish cedar. It provides critical support and transmits sound vibrations from the instrument's top to its bottom.

Clothespins are used to gently clamp the lining in place. Care must be taken not to scratch or dent the rosewood sides.

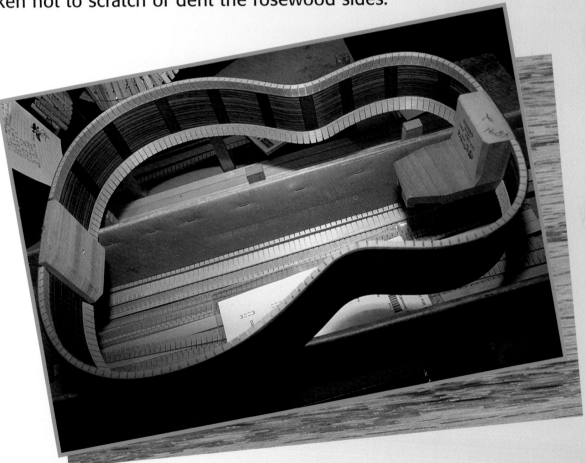

1.

2.

3.

SIX GENERATIONS OF GUITARS: THE MARTIN TIMELINE

1833 *Christian Frederick Martin, Sr.[1] leaves his home in Germany and moves to New York City. He quickly sets up a guitar-making and music shop on the city's Lower West Side.*

1838 *C.F. Martin, Sr. sells his business in New York and moves with his wife and family to an 8-acre property in Nazareth, Pennsylvania. It is here that the company will grow and flourish.*

1867 *With the death of C.F. Martin Sr., the company is headed by his son, C.F. Martin, Jr.[2] Continued growth in sales requires expansion of the factory with more than a dozen workers.*

Who's Who:
1. C.F. Martin Sr. 2. C.F. Martin, Jr.
3. Frank Henry Martin 4. C.F. Martin III
5. Frank Herbert Martin 6. C.F. Martin IV

1888 *The unexpected death of C.F. Martin Jr. places the company's future in the hands of his 22-year-old son, Frank[3]. Within a few years, Martin is doing its own distribution and is experiencing a great boost in sales. By 1898, the company is producing about 220 guitars per year and about 113 mandolins.*

1948 *Frank Henry Martin dies, leaving control of the company to C.F. Martin III[4]. In 1955, his son—Frank Herbert Martin[5]—joins the company and later takes over the presidency in 1970.*

1986 *Christian "Chris" Frederick Martin IV[6]— the sixth generation Martin—takes his place as the head of Martin Guitar Company. By 1998, the company is producing more than 50,000 guitars per year, in more than 50 models.*

4.

5.

6.

Tops and Backs

When the Spanish cedar lining has dried, the frame is fitted with a top and a back.

The top—made of spruce—is also called the "soundboard." That is because it is the surface that will vibrate when the strings are plucked. This will "pump" the sound waves out the sound hole.

Braces must be placed on the inside of the soundboard to keep the guitar from collapsing once it is strung. A special "X"-bracing pattern (designed by founder C.F. Martin Sr.) is attached. The bracing pieces are glued in place and a vacuum press holds them until they set.

A special X-bracing pattern is glued to the soundboard and held in place by a vacuum press.

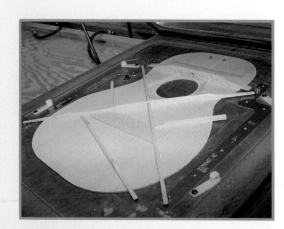

16

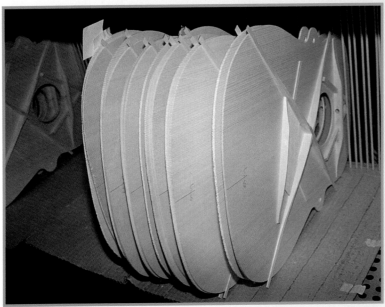

X-braced soundboards wait to be fitted to a body.

Brace Shaping

After gluing, the soundboard goes to a skilled craftsperson for brace shaping. This is a process of shaving and shaping the wood braces with a chisel. Many Martin models have "scalloped" braces where the middle of the braces are scooped or "scalloped."

Scalloping is done by hand with a series of wooden chisels.

17

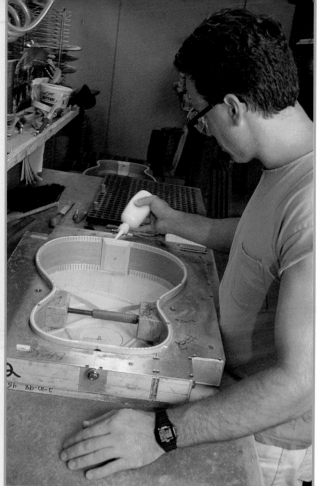

Above: Glue is applied to the edge of the guitar's rim before the soundboard is added.
Right: The guitar's rim is flipped over and glued before the back is applied.

Top and Back Go On

The soundboard is the first big piece to be attached to the body rim. The notched lining on the frame is opened to accept the bracing ends. Once these pieces are fitted together, the soundboard is glued to the frame.

The guitar's back goes on much the same way as the front. When the back is in place, it is glued and held in a press. The press applies even pressure so the glue dries and holds evenly.

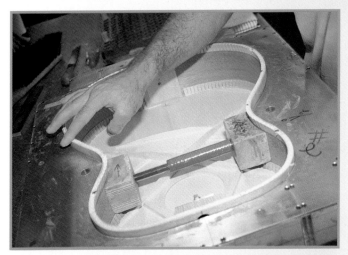

Sidenotes

In 1993, Martin introduced a special new kind of "mini" guitar called the Backpacker. With a smaller body shape and a shortened neck, it is designed to go anywhere. Since its introduction, the Backpacker has been taken to the top of Mount Everest and to the North and South Poles. It was also the first guitar in space (it was taken on the *Columbia* space shuttle)!

Above left: *The glue is spread out evenly before applying the back.*
Left: *Placing the back onto the body.*
Below: *Once it is assembled and clamped, the body is shelved until it is completely dry.*

19

"Purfling"

To protect and seal the edges of the instrument, a special binding called purfling is attached. The edging is also a decorative element that adds to the overall beauty of the finished product.

After the purfling is glued, it is taped to hold it in place. Then the entire body is wrapped with cloth strapping (strips) until the glue dries completely.

Purfling is glued and taped in place.

Nearly finished bodies with purfling in place.

When all the purfling is glued, cloth strapping secures the pieces.

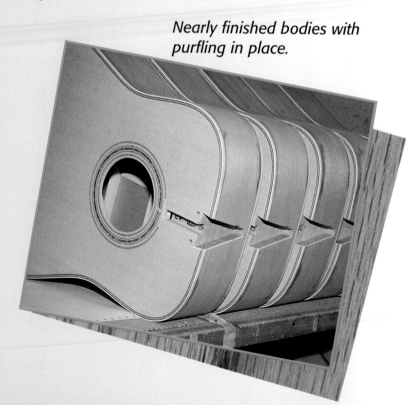

Above: Rough-cut necks.
Right: Shaping the neck with a tool called a wood rasp.

Working on the Neck

The neck is made from a solid piece of mahogany. It is cut into shape by a special blade that is programmed by a computer. The computer makes sure every neck is cut to exact specifications.

After the rough shape is cut, a skilled craftsperson shapes it with a drawknife and a rasp. These are some of the oldest carpentry tools. Drawknives were used by Colonial craftsmen in the 1700s to shape wagon wheels.

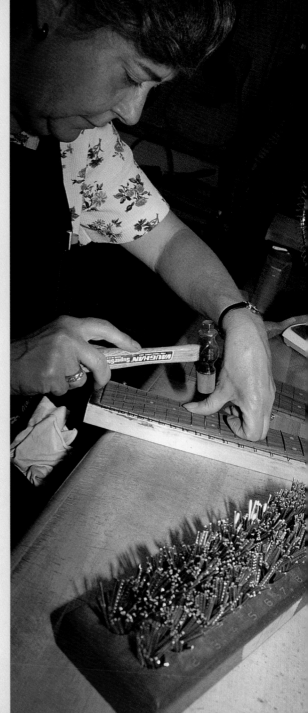

Frets are inserted into pre-cut grooves in the fingerboard.

Necks and Inlays

Next, a steel support is placed inside the neck. The rod works against the tension created when the instrument is strung. Once the rod is in place, it is glued and covered by the fingerboard.

For the more expensive models, fingerboards are decorated with special inlaid designs. Most of these designs are made with Mother of Pearl or abalone pearl.

Above: *Glue is applied over the steel rod in preparation for the fingerboard.*
Below: *The fingerboard is applied.*

A nearly finished neck.

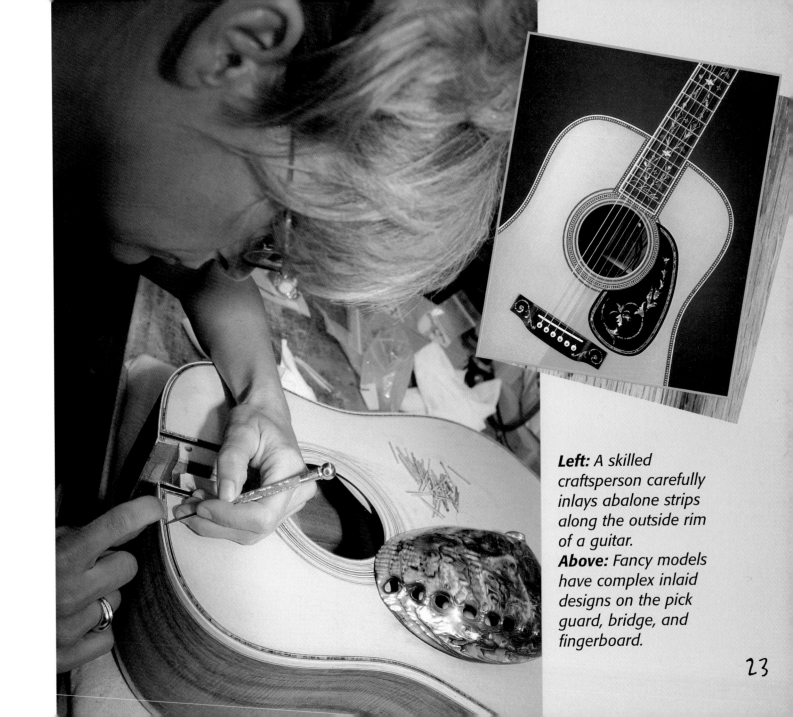

Left: A skilled craftsperson carefully inlays abalone strips along the outside rim of a guitar.

Above: Fancy models have complex inlaid designs on the pick guard, bridge, and fingerboard.

23

Putting a Neck on a Body

Before the neck and the body come together for good, they are first pre-fitted. A tight fit is very important to the overall sound of the instrument. That's because the neck absorbs and "flavors" the sound from the guitar body. To work properly, the neck must be centered perfectly onto the body.

The neck joint is made to fit so well that the neck could stay on without any glue. But glue is added when the pieces are put together permanently. Once fitted, the neck and body are numbered so they can be finished separately.

Special chisels, carving knives, and saws are used to fit the neck to the body.

When the neck is attached, it must be perfectly centered over the body.

Polishing after many coats of laquer have been applied.

Sanding the surface before more laquer coats are applied.

Bodywork and Other Elements

There are more than 20 steps required to finish the body. Because wood has microscopic pockets in its surface (it is porous), the surface is filled with a wood paste to smooth it. It is sprayed and sanded many times and finally polished in a careful series of steps.

As the body is finished, the tuning gears are attached to the head stock (top of the neck).

When both the body and neck are ready, they are re-united. Their fit is checked once again before they are glued together permanently.

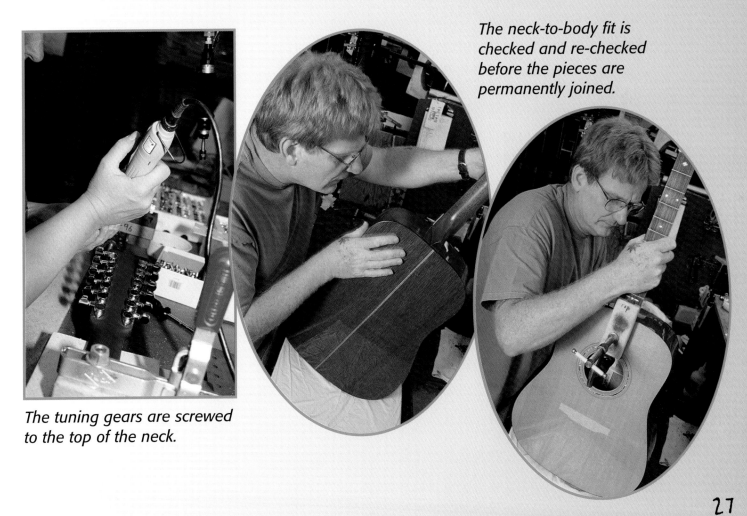

The neck-to-body fit is checked and re-checked before the pieces are permanently joined.

The tuning gears are screwed to the top of the neck.

STARS AND GUITARS

In recent years, Martin has developed a line of limited edition guitars called the "Signature Series." These special guitars are designed for, developed, and approved by music legends. Each is decorated with unique inlay designs and each fingerboard is inlaid with the musician's signature.

Notable signature models include the N-20WN Willie Nelson Limited Edition, which is a close replica of the guitar he named "Trigger." Another special model is the Don McLean edition, with words from his legendary song "American Pie" inlaid in the fingerboard. The Stephen Stills guitar has stars inlaid in the pick guard. A special edition guitar was created for Eric Clapton after his performance on MTV's "Unplugged." It is now one of the company's most popular models.

Martin has also created some very unique guitars for its customers. One guitar had a fingerboard with the "Lord's Prayer" inlaid in Mother of Pearl.

One of the most expensive custom guitars Martin ever made was produced for country superstar Travis Tritt. That guitar cost about $36,000!

Rock superstar Eric Clapton has two signature models to his name.

Paul Simon with his signature edition OM-42PS.

Martin's artist relations director, Dick Boak, shows off the N-20WN next to Willie Nelson and the orginal guitar that inspired the Martin model.

29

Building a Bridge

The bridge holds the ball ends of the strings in place below the sound hole. It also plays an important part in transferring vibrations to the guitar's soundboard. Most Martin bridges are made from ebony or rosewood.

Before the bridge is attached, the shiny finish must be removed from the gluing area on the soundboard. This creates a better surface for gluing.

Staining the bridge.

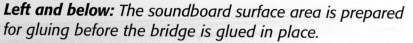

Left and below: *The soundboard surface area is prepared for gluing before the bridge is glued in place.*

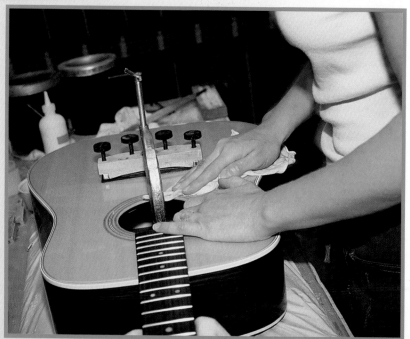

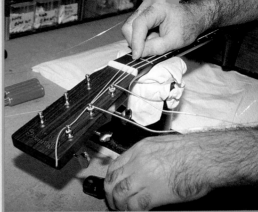

Right: A bundle of strings is checked for quality.
Far right, top and middle: Stringing and tuning the instrument.
Far right bottom: Guitars sit in a rack while they wait for final inspection.

String 'Em Up

After the bridge is added, the guitar's parts are nearly complete. Now the instrument is strung. An experienced stringer attaches the strings and tunes the guitar. The instrument is then play-tested. It is also carefully inspected to make sure there are no imperfections.

The new guitar will now sit on a shelf for a few weeks. This will allow the guitar to "settle in." After this period, the instrument will be play-tested and inspected again. If it passes inspection, it will be shipped out to one of thousands of music stores around the world.

Glossary

Flourish to grow and prosper.

Inlay to set a decorative pattern into a surface or ground material.

Kerf a slit or notch made by a saw or cutting torch.

Microscopic something that can only be seen by a microscope.

Purfling ornaments on the edge of something.

Soundboard a thin board placed in some instruments to reinforce its tones.

Vibration movement from side to side.

For More Information

BOOKS

Ardley, Neil. David King. Phillip Dowell. *Music* (Eyewitness Books). New York, NY: Knopf, 1989.

Jones, George. *My First Book of How Things Are Made: Crayons, Jeans, Guitars, Peanut Butter, and More* (Cartwheel Learning Bookshelf). New York, NY: Cartwheel Books, 1995.

Kain, Kathleen. Robert Byrd (Illustrator). *All About How Things Are Made* (Inspector McQ). Chicago, IL: World Book, Inc., 1995.

Scholastic Reference. *Musical Instruments: From Flutes Carved of Bone, to Lutes, to Modern Electric Guitars* (Scholastic Voyages of Discovery). New York, NY: Scholastic, 1994.

WEB SITE

Martin Guitars Learn the history of the company, read the online magazine, and take a tour of the guitar museum—www.mguitar.com.

Index